"TEACH ME YOUR WAYS, O LORD,
THAT I MAY LIVE ACCORDING
TO YOUR TRUTH!"

Psalm 86:11

HOW TO USE THIS BOOK

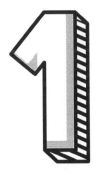

Set aside time each day to discover...study... enjoy... learn... God's Word. You can study/write each verse in one day, or take several days to complete the "lesson."

First, look up the Scripture verse in your Bible.

 Matthew 19:14

QUICK TIPS Try to understand the <u>context</u> of the Scripture by reading a couple verses before and after the verse listed.

Trace the letters in the Bible verse.

'Let the children come to me. Don't stop them!"

Write the verse on your own.

"Let the children come

 If writing the entire verse is too difficult for your child, pick out a couple words for them to write instead.

HOW TO USE THIS BOOK

 Draw a picture to illustrate the verse.

 When you illustrate the verse, it helps you take the time to understand what the verse means and how it can apply to your life.

 Sing the words of the Scripture to the tune of the song listed. When we sing something, it helps us remember! By putting the verse to song (and adding some actions), memorization will be fun and easy.

Let the children come	(the farmer in the dell)
Let the children come	(the farmer in the dell)
To Jesus	(hi ho the dairy-O)
Don't stop them	(the farmer in the dell)

 It helps if you hum the tune to the song first to get the tempo and tune. Then sing the words in a way that fits.

For example, this line would be sung:
"Tooo oo oo Jeeesus" (hi ho the dairy-O)

 Drawing and singing helps kids enjoy learning! Let this be a time where you participate with them in being creative and moving around.

Matthew 19:14

"Let the children come
to me. Don't stop them!"

WRITE

 Draw a picture to illustrate this verse.

 "Let the children come to me. Don't stop them!"
Matthew 19:14
Sing the verse to the tune of "The Farmer in the Dell".

Let the children come   (the farmer in the dell)
Let the children come   (the farmer in the dell)
To Jesus   (hi ho the dairy-O)
Don't stop them   (the farmer in the dell)

Romans 8:38

"Nothing can ever
separate us from God's
love."

 Draw a picture to illustrate this verse.

 "Nothing can ever separate us from God's love."

Romans 8:38

Sing the verse to the tune of "London Bridges"

Nothing can separate	(London Bridges)
Us from	(falling down)
God's love	(falling down)
Nothing can separate	(London Bridges)
Us from	(falling down)
God's love	(my fair lady)

Proverbs 3:5

"Trust in the Lord with all your heart."

 Draw a picture to illustrate this verse.

 "Trust in the Lord with all your heart." Proverbs 3:5

Sing the verse to the tune of "Ring Around the Rosie".

Trust in the Lord   (ring around the rosie)

With all your heart (pocket full of posie)

Proverbs 3   (ashes ashes)

Verse 5   (we all fall down)

John 3:36

"Anyone who believes in God's Son has eternal life."

 **DRAW** Draw a picture to illustrate this verse.

(Eternal life means that you are going to live with God forever.)

 **SING** Anyone who believes in God's Son has eternal life."

John 3:36

Sing the verse to the tune of "Row Row Row Your Boat".

Anyone	(row row row your boat)
Who believes	(gently down the stream)
In	(merrily merrily)
God's Son	(merrily merrily)
Has eternal life	(life is but a dream)

John 14:6

"Jesus told him, 'I am
the way, the truth, and
the life.'"

Draw a picture to illustrate this verse.

"Jesus told him, 'I am the way, the truth, and the life."
John 14:6

Sing the verse to the tune of "The Wheels on the Bus"

Jesus told him	(The Wheels on the bus)
I am the way	(go round and round)
I am the truth	(round and round)
I am the life	(round and round)
Jesus told him	(The Wheels on the bus)
I am the way	(go round and round)
The truth and the life	(all through the town)

Psalm 23:1

"The Lord is my shepherd;

I have all that I need."

 Draw a picture to illustrate this verse.

 "The Lord is my Shepherd; I have all that I need."
Psalm 23:1

Sing the verse to the tune of "Bingo"

The Lord is my Shepherd (There was a farmer had a dog)
I have all that I need   (and Bingo was his name, oh)
Psalm 23:1   (B I N G O)
Psalm 23:1   (B I N G O)
Psalm 23:1   (B I N G O)
I have all that I need!   (and Bingo was his name)

READ Genesis 50:20

TRACE

"...but God intended it
all for good."

WRITE

 Draw a picture to illustrate this verse.

 "...but God intended it all for good." Genesis 50:20

Sing the verse to the tune of "The Ants Go Marching One By One"

But God intended it for good (the ants go marching one by one)
Hurrah, hurrah
But God intended it for good (the ants go marching one by one)
Hurrah, hurrah
But God intended it for good (the little one stopped to suck his thumb)
But God intended it for good (and they all go marching down)
Genesis 50:20 (and they all go marching down)
50:20 (to the ground)

Exodus 12:13

"When I see the blood,

I will pass over you."

 Draw a picture to illustrate this verse.

 "When I see the blood, I will pass over you." Exodus 12:13

Sing the verse to the tune of "Row Row Row Your Boat".

When I see the blood   (row row row your boat)

I will pass over you   (gently down the stream)

Exodus 12   (merrily merrily merrily merrily)

Verse 14   (life is but a dream)

Genesis 1:1

"In the beginning God
created the heavens
and the earth."

WRITE

Draw a picture to illustrate this verse.

"In the beginning God created the heavens and the earth." Genesis 1:1

Sing the verse to the tune of "Skip to My Lou"

In the beginning   (Skip, skip, skip to my Lou)
God created   (Skip, skip, skip to my Lou)
The heavens   (Skip, skip, skip to my Lou)
And the earth   (Skip to my Lou, my darlin')

Psalm 118:24

"This is the day the Lord

has made. We will

rejoice and be glad in it."

 **Draw a picture to illustrate this verse.**

"This is the day the Lord has made. We will rejoice and be glad in it." Psalm 118:24

 Sing the verse to the tune of "Here We Go 'Round the Mulberry Bush".

This is the day	(Here we go 'round)
The Lord has made	(the mulberry bush)
The Lord has made	(the mulberry bush)
The Lord has made	(the mulberry bush)
This is the day	(Here we go 'round)
The Lord has made	(the mulberry bush)
We will rejoice	(on a cold and frosty morning)

I Samuel 16:7

"People judge by outward appearance, but the Lord looks at the heart."

Draw a picture to illustrate this verse.

"People judge by outward appearance, but the Lord looks at the heart." 1 Samuel 16:7

Sing the verse to the tune of "The Farmer in the Dell"

The Lord looks at the heart   (the farmer in the dell)

The Lord looks at the heart   (the farmer in the dell)

People see the outside   (hi ho the dairy oh)

But the Lord looks at the heart (the farmer in the dell)

Psalm 121:2

"My help comes from the
Lord, who made heaven
and earth."

 Draw a picture to illustrate this verse.

 "My help comes from the Lord, who made heaven
and earth! Psalm 121:2
Sing the verse to the tune of "Do You Know the Muffin Man?"

My help comes from the Lord (Do you know the muffin man)
From the Lord   (the muffin man)
From the Lord   (the muffin man)
My help comes from the Lord (Do you know the muffin man)
Who made heaven and earth! (Who lives on Drury Lane)

Romans 8:11

"The Spirit of God, who
raised Jesus from the
dead, lives in you."

 Draw a picture to illustrate this verse.

 "The Spirit of God, who raised Jesus from the dead, lives in you." Romans 8:11

Sing the verse to the tune of "The Wheels on the Bus"

The Spirit of God	(The Wheels on the bus)
Who raised Jesus	(go round and round)
From the dead	(round and round
From the dead	(round and round)
The Spirit of God	(The Wheels on the bus)
Who raised Jesus	(go round and round)
Lives in you	(all through the town)

Psalm 119:105

"Your word is a lamp to guide my feet and a light for my path."

 Draw a picture to illustrate this verse.

 Your word is a lamp to guide my feet and a light for my path." Psalm 119:105

Sing the verse to the tune of "Skip to My Lou"

Your Word is a lamp   (Skip, skip, skip to my Lou)
Your Word is a lamp   (Skip, skip, skip to my Lou)
Your Word is a lamp   (Skip, skip, skip to my Lou)
To guide my feet   (Skip to my Lou, my darlin')

Romans 3:22

"We are made right with

God by placing our faith

in Jesus Christ."

WRITE

 **Draw a picture to illustrate this verse.**

 "We are made right with God by placing our faith in Jesus Christ." Romans 3:22

Sing the verse to the tune of "I've been working on the Railroad"

We are made right with God	(I've been working on the railroad)
By placing our faith	(all the live long day)
In Jesus Christ	(I've been working on the railroad)
Romans 3:22	(just to pass the time away)
We are made right with God	(Can't you hear the whistle blowing)
By placing our faith	(Rise up so early in the morn)
In Jesus Christ	(Can't you hear the whistle blowing)
Romans 3:22	(Dinah blow your horn)

READ

James 4:8

TRACE

"Come close to God, and
God will come close to you."

WRITE

 **Draw a picture to illustrate this verse.**

SING

"Come close to God, and God will come close to you.
James 4:8

Sing the verse to the tune of "Hickory Dickory Dock"

Come close to God   (Hickory dickory dock)

Come close to God   (the mouse ran up the clock)

And God will   (the clock struck one)

Come close   (the mouse ran down)

to you   (hickory dickory dock)

READ

Luke 19:10

TRACE

"The Son of Man came
to seek and save those
who are lost."

WRITE

 **Draw a picture to illustrate this verse.**

 "The Son of Man came to seek and save those who are lost." Luke 19:10

Sing the verse to the tune of "The Farmer in the Dell".

The Son of Man came   (the farmer in the dell)
To seek and to save   (the farmer in the dell)
Those who are lost   (hi ho the dairy-O)
Luke 19:10   (the farmer in the dell)

Psalm 86:5

TRACE

"O Lord, you are so good,
so ready to forgive."

WRITE

 **Draw a picture to illustrate this verse.**

 "O Lord, you are so good, so ready to forgive..."

Psalm 86:5

Sing the verse to the tune of "Jesus Loves Me".

O Lord, you are so good	(Jesus loves me this I know)
So ready to forgive	(for the Bible tells me so)
O Lord, you are so good	(little ones to him belong)
So ready to forgive	(they are weak but he is strong)
Lord you are so good	(yes, Jesus loves me)
Lord you are so good	(yes, Jesus loves me)
Lord you are so good	(yes, Jesus loves me)
Psalm 86:5	(the Bible tells me so)

READ Matthew 28:6

TRACE

"He is risen from the
dead, just as he said
would happen."

WRITE

 **Draw a picture to illustrate this verse.**

 "He is risen from the dead, just as he said would happen." Matthew 28:6

Sing the verse to the tune of "Hallelujah"

He is risen	(Hallelujah!)
From the dead	(Hallelujah!)
Just as	(Hallelujah!)
He said	(Hallelujah!)
Would happen	(Hall le lu jah!)

TRACE

"This is the message of
Good News...--that there
is peace with God
through Jesus Christ."

WRITE

 **Draw a picture to illustrate this verse.**

 "This is the message of Good News...--that there is peace with God through Jesus Christ...." Acts 10:36

Sing the verse to the tune of "If You're Happy and You Know It"

This is the message of Good News

   (If you're happy and you know it clap your hands)

This is the message of Good News

   (If you're happy and you know it clap your hands)

That there is peace

   (if you're happy and you know it)

With God through Jesus Christ

   (then your face will surely show it)

This is the message of Good News

   (If you're happy and you know it clap your hands)

TRACE

"Holy, holy, holy is the
Lord God, the Almighty."

WRITE

Draw a picture to illustrate this verse.

Holy means perfect, pure, worthy to be worshipped and to stand in awe of.

Holy, holy, holy is the Lord God, the Almighty...."

Revelation 4:8

You can sing the song

"Holy, holy, holy, Lord God Almighty".

(You can find this on You-Tube if you aren't familiar with it.)

Matthew 1:23

TRACE

"They will call him

Immanuel, which means

"God is with us.'"

WRITE

 Draw a picture to illustrate this verse.

 "...they will call him Immanuel, which means 'God is with us' " Matthew 1:23

Sing to the tune of "Jingle Bells"

They will	(Jingle Bells)
Call him	(Jingle Bells)
Immanuel	(Jingle all the way)
Which	(Oh what fun)
Means	(it is to ride)
God is with us!	(in a one horse open sleigh!)

READ

TRACE

"Don't be afraid. Just
have faith."

WRITE

 Draw a picture to illustrate this verse.

[blank drawing box]

 "Don't be afraid. Just have faith...." Luke 8:50

Sing the verse to the tune of "Twinkle Twinkle Little Star"

Don't be afraid	(Twinkle twinkle)
Just have faith	(little star)
Don't be afraid	(how I wonder)
Just have faith	(what you are)
Don't be afraid	(Up above the)
Just have faith	(world so high)
Luke 8:50	(like a diamond in the sky)
Don't be afraid	(Twinkle twinkle)
Just have faith	(little star)
Luke 8:50	(how I wonder what you are)

Philippians 4:6

"Don't worry about
anything; instead, pray
about everything."

 Draw a picture to illustrate this verse.

 "Don't worry about anything; instead, pray about everything." Philippians 4:6

Sing the verse to the tune of "Jesus Loves Me"

Don't worry about anything   (Jesus loves me this I know)

Instead pray about everything   (for the Bible tells me so)

Don't worry about anything   (Jesus loves me this I know)

Instead pray about everything   (for the Bible tells me so)

Don't worry   (Yes, Jesus loves me)

Don't worry   (Yes, Jesus loves me)

Don't worry   (Yes, Jesus loves me)

Philippians 4:6   (The Bible tells me so)

READ Hebrews 13:16

TRACE

"Don't forget to do good and to share with those in need."

WRITE

 Draw a picture to illustrate this verse.

"Don't forget to do good and to share with those in need."
Hebrews 13:16

 Sing the verse to the tune of "Row Row Row Your Boat"

Don't forget to do   (Row row row your boat)
Good and to share   (gently down the stream)
With those in need   (Merrily merrily merrily merrily)
Hebrews 13:16   (Life is but a dream)

HERE IS A LIST OF SIMPLE MELODIES TO HELP YOU KEEP SINGING AND MEMORIZING GOD'S WORD:

Are you sleeping?
Baa Baa Black Sheep
Deep and Wide
His Banner Over Me is Love
Itsy, Bitsy Spider
I've Got the Joy Joy Joy Joy
Jesus Loves the Little Children
My God is so Big
Oh How I love Jesus
Our God is an Awesome God
Row, Row, Row Your Boat
Do You Know the Muffin Man?
God is so Good
Silent Night
The B-I-B-L-E
The Hokey Pokey
The Wheels on the Bus
Three Blind Mice
This Little Light of Mine
Twinkle, Twinkle Little Star
ABC Song

Away in a Manger
Darling Clementine
Do Your Ears Hang Low
If You're Happy and You Know it
I've Been Working on the Railroad
Jesus Loves Me
London Bridge
O Come All Ye Faithful
Old McDonald Had a Farm
Praise Him, Praise Him
Seek Ye First
Farmer in the Dell
Head, Shoulders, Knees, and Toes
Hickory Dickory Dock
Skip to My Lou
The Mulberry Bush
There's a Hole in the Bucket
This is the Day the Lord Has Made
This Old Man
Trust and Obey
Where, Oh Where, has my Little Dog Gone

If you need tools to help your children grow in
their walk with the Lord, use this QR Code to go to

DIGGINGINTOGOD.COM

60010093R00033